i ♥ my Petals

Photography: Nick Karras

Text: Sayaka Adachi

Design: Jesse Karras

Crystal River Publishing

To place an order, go to ilovemypetals.com

ISBN 0-9743562-9-8

To the truly brave women
who dare to love their petals
in their full uniqueness

Contents

Introduction - 1

Photography and Quotes - 2

Petals History - 62

Why we published this book - 65

Who modeled for the photos? - 67

Anatomy and Physiology - 68

Petals Diagram - 68

Scent and Taste - 74

How to Keep the Petals Happy - 75

Petals Problems - 77

Want More? - 78

Introduction

Welcome to a journey into a woman's secret anatomy, her vulva. It's not every day we get to see so many varieties of vulvas. So join us—take a deep breath, linger a bit, and notice the subtle and not so subtle differences among these beautiful vulvas. This book is not meant to represent "all" vulva types and shapes. If you don't find one that looks like yours, don't worry. Vulvas are like faces. We are all unique, no two are alike.

It is our sincere hope that you find these images empowering and that you love your own vulva. We call them Petals, as they are just like flower petals, each with distinct beauty and characteristic scents, and we want to honor each one.

We hope you'll join the many women around the world who bravely declare:

"I Love My Petals"!

"If we could see the miracle of a single flower clearly,

our whole life would change."

~Buddha

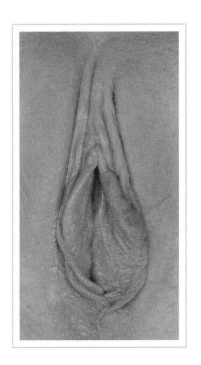 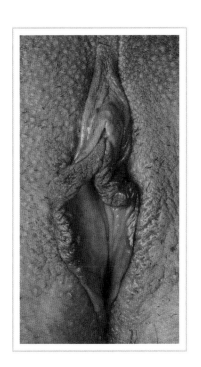 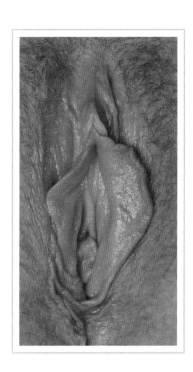

3

"I finally realized that being grateful to my body

was key to giving more love to myself."

~Oprah Winfrey

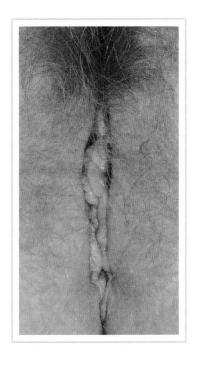 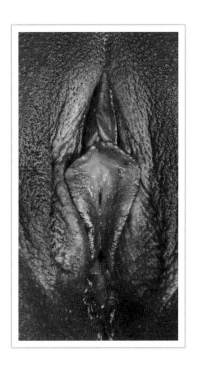 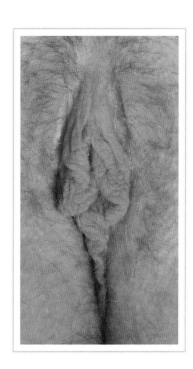

"I feel there is something unexplored about a woman that only a woman can explore"

~Georgia O'Keefe

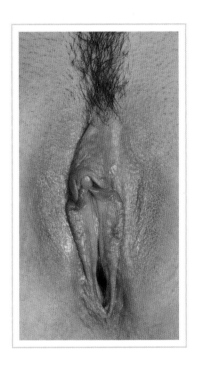 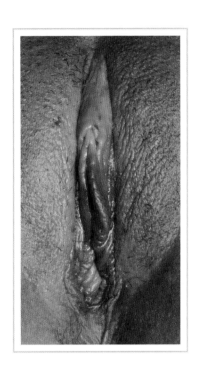 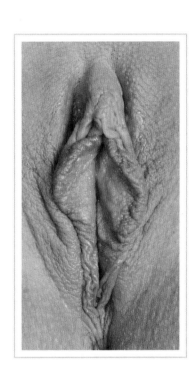

"You can't build joy on a feeling of self-loathing."

~Ram Dass

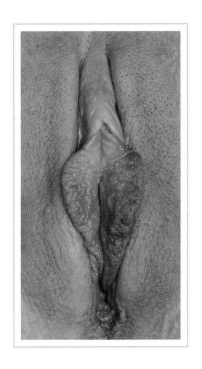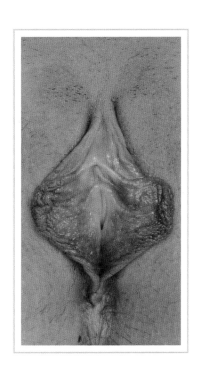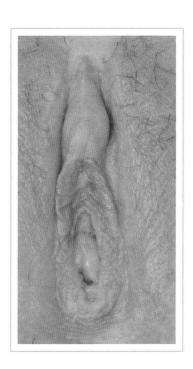

"While beautiful and intriguing, my petals are

confident and powerful. I know that I can use them

to get what I want,

but more importantly, I know that I don't have to use

them for anything that does not make me happy."

~Petals Model

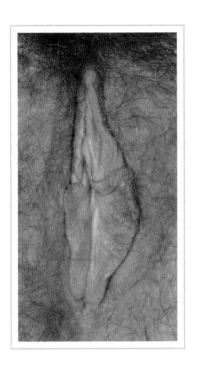 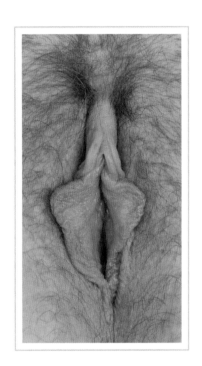 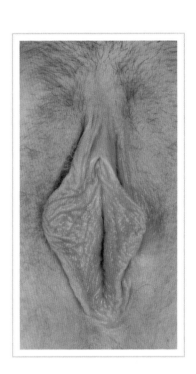

"There came a time when the risk to remain tight in the bud was more painful than the risk it took to blossom."

~Anaïs Nin

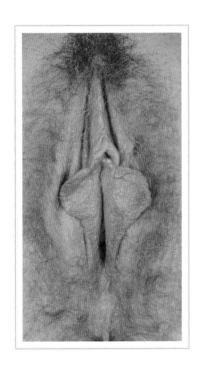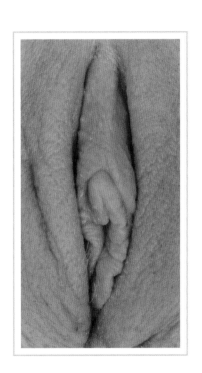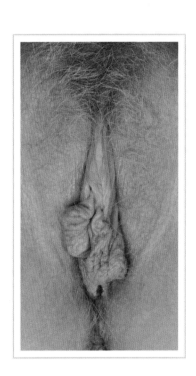

"Like many other girls, I hated my body and I had an eating disorder. Someone gave me the Petals and it made me cry. I looked at myself and eventually saw beauty. Now, I see that all of me can be beautiful, in my unique shape and curves."

~Petals Model

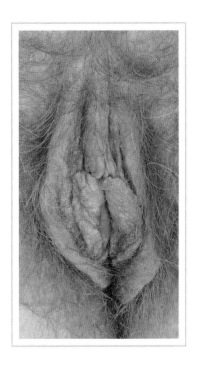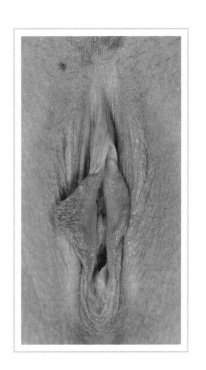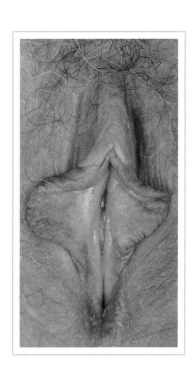

"I am my own experiment. I am my own work of art."

~Madonna

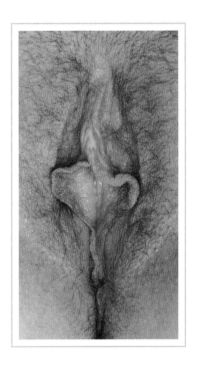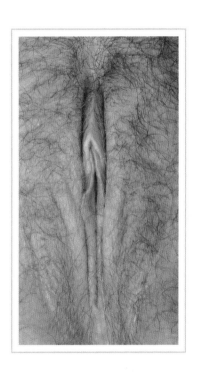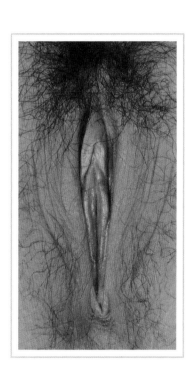

Lovely sweet petals

so soft and sweet

Perfect and precious

each one so very unique

The art of a woman

finally discovered

Much Power

Much vulnerability lies within

Yet your admiration and desire

is our only hope

~Poem by Tara

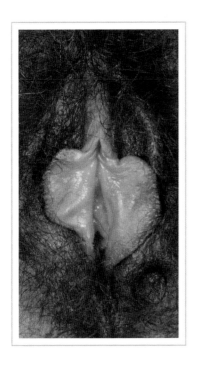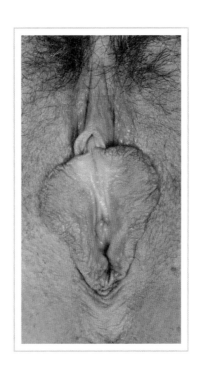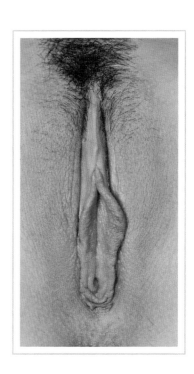

"The most adventurous journey to embark on;

is the journey to yourself, the most exciting thing to

discover; is who you really are, the most treasured

pieces that you can find; are all the pieces of you,

the most special portrait you can recognize; is the

portrait of your soul."

~C. JoyBell C.

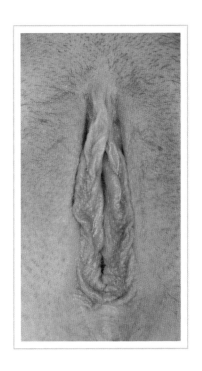 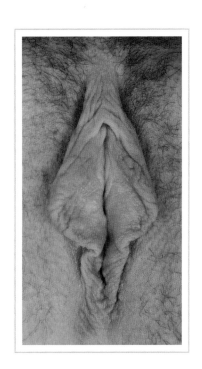 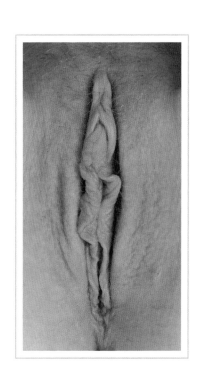

21

"When I modeled for this book, someone told me that my petals looked like an orchid. Now every time I see an orchid, I think about my time in front of the camera, feeling appreciated and accepted."

~Petals Model

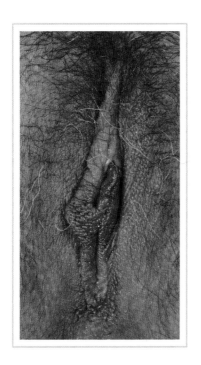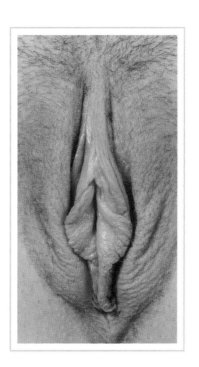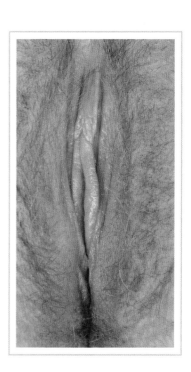

23

"If only I'd known my differentness would be an asset,

then my earlier life would have been much easier."

~Bette Midler

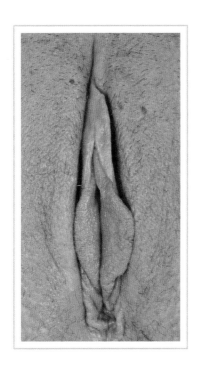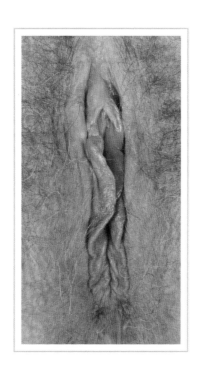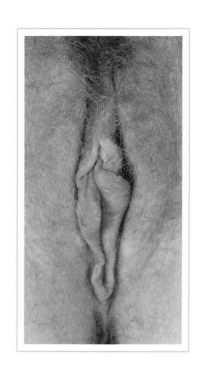

"Twelve years ago, I was attacked and raped

leaving me deaf, barren, horribly scarred and

hating my body. Then I met a woman who saw

past the box-knife scars and chose to only ever see

the petals of my flower. With skilled fingers she

reached into me and rejoined the broken threads

of my feminine core. My mother once told me that

much of the pain women endure in life is centered

in this most amazing of places and yet it is often

the last place we look for solutions. Fortunately,

someone helped me to look in the right place,

by unfolding my petals!"

~Petals Fan

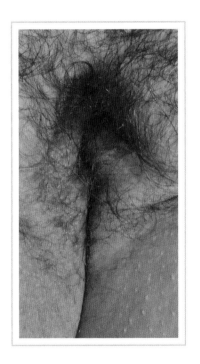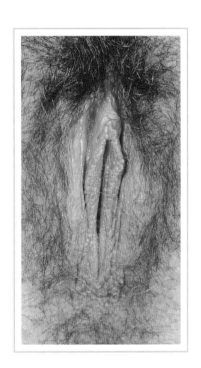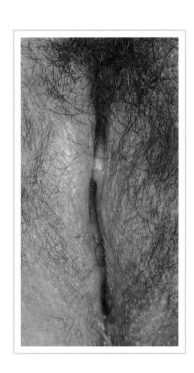

"Anything you want to ask a teacher, ask yourself, and wait for the answer in silence."

~Byron Katie

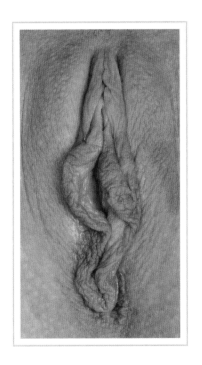 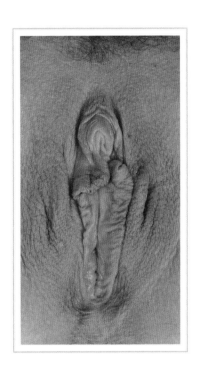 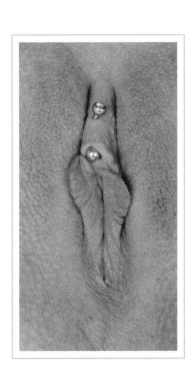

"A photo shoot unlike any other, so truly adoring of

my body evoked a sad realization that my petals

had not been fully adored by another in many

years. I thought how wonderful it is that at least

one perspective viewpoint has been captured on

film and will live on to inspire, educate, excite,

open, remind, and perhaps even release another,

for eternity. Thank you for allowing me to share

– it is a true honor."

~Petals Model

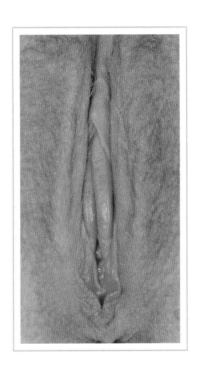 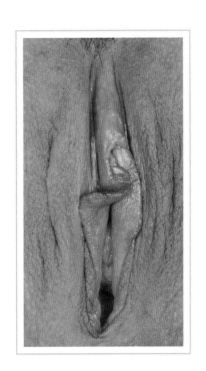 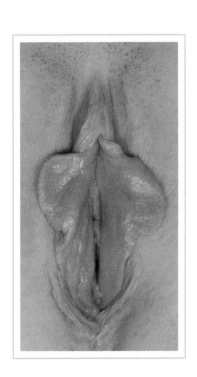

"You're incredibly, absolutely, extremely, supremely,

unbelievably different."

~Kami Garcia, Beautiful Creatures

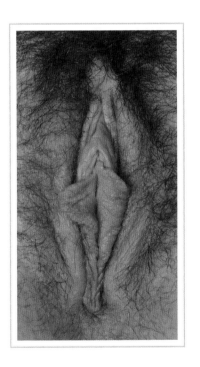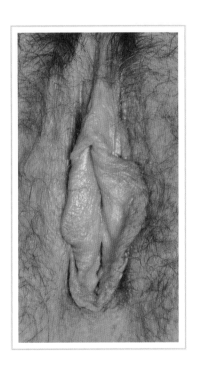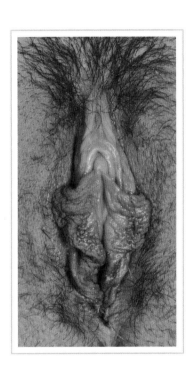

33

"It is at the edge of a petal that love awaits."

~William Carlos Williams

(American Poet, 1883-1963)

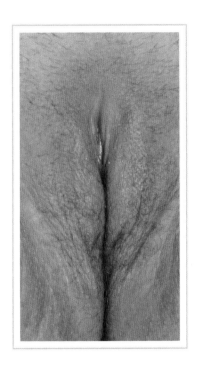

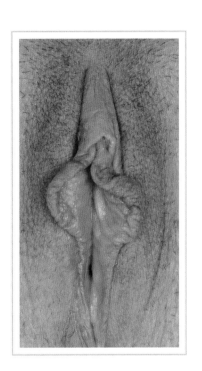

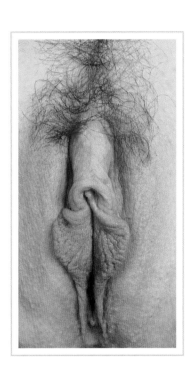

"Think how lucky you are that the skin you live in,

so beautifully holds the "You" who's within."

~Michael Tyler, The Skin You Live In

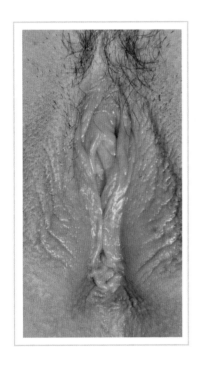  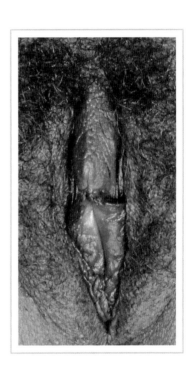

"I used to have a very ambivalent relationship with my yoni. As a little girl, I was made to feel guilty about touching my genitals, but I couldn't help myself as there was so much pleasure. Inevitably, I would feel guilty, and I carried this guilt and shame into all my relationships. When I learned about sacred sexuality in mid-life, I slowly became friends with my yoni. Now, it is my passion to help men and women celebrate, respect, and honor this sacred space."

~Joan Heartfield, Ph.D

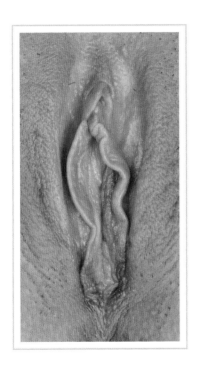 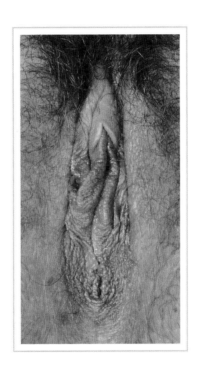 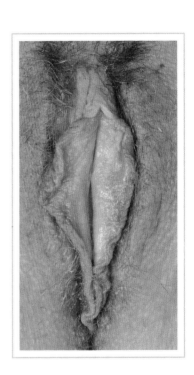

"Art is not the application of a canon of beauty but what the instinct and the brain can conceive beyond any canon. When we love a woman we don't start measuring her limbs."

~Pablo Picasso

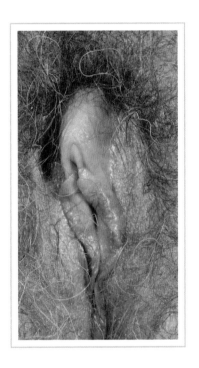 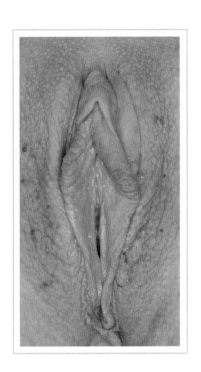 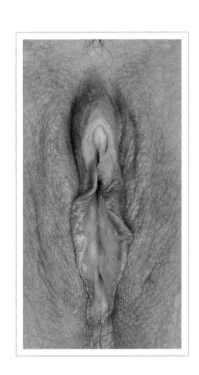

41

"My ex-boyfriend once called my petals a pastrami sandwich. I was so embarrassed that all I could think of was to cut them off. I am so glad I didn't, because now, I know my petals are beautiful and also delicious!"

~Petals Model

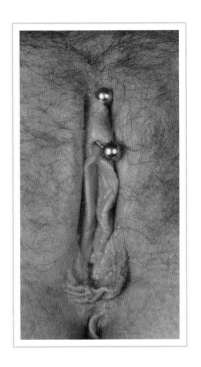
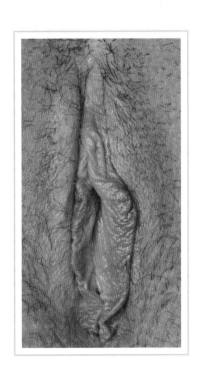
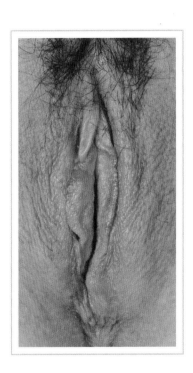

"You are imperfect, permanently and inevitably

flawed. And you are beautiful."

~Amy Bloom

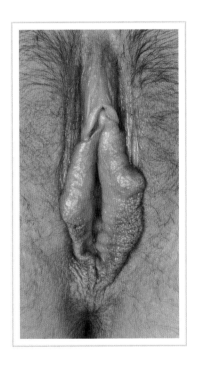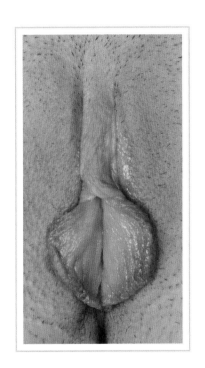

"I never saw my pussy as being something that could be seen as beautiful or visually appreciated until I was told by a little Thai woman doing my Brazilian wax that I have a pretty pussy. Since then, I have been pretty damn proud of my goodies!"

~Petals Model

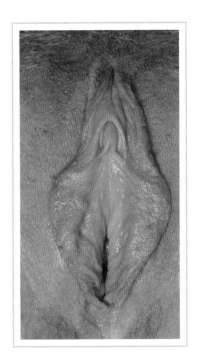 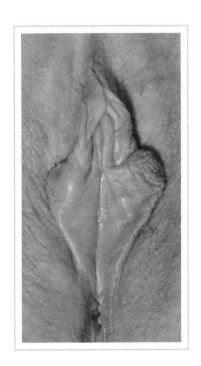 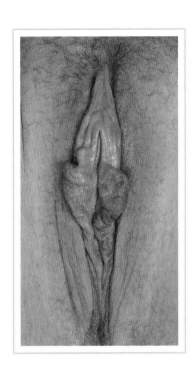

"Within my body are all the sacred places of the world, and the most profound pilgrimage I can ever make is within my own body."

~Saraha

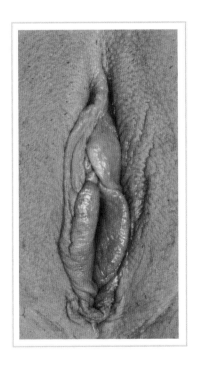 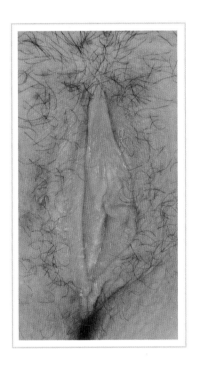 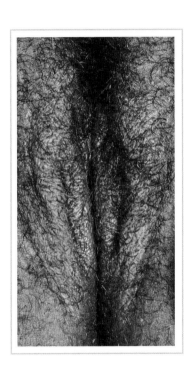

"When I got diagnosed with herpes, I thought my life was over. Now, thanks to it, I take care of myself better, and I now have a much closer relationship with my petals."

~Petals Model

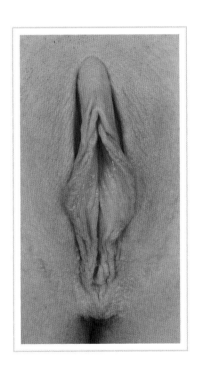
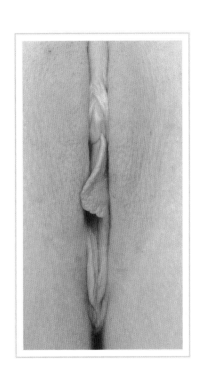
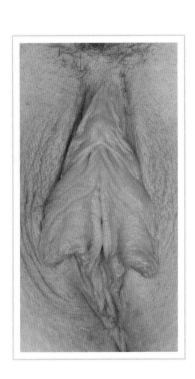

"Be yourself. The world worships an original."

~Ingrid Bergman

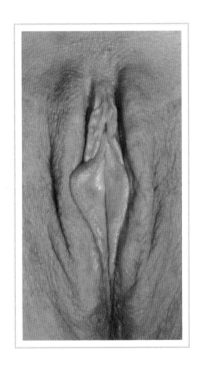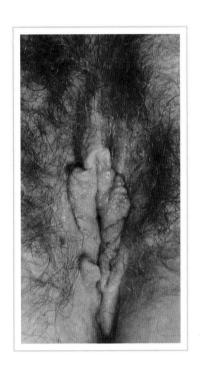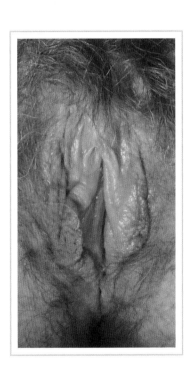

"If God had wanted us to be the same,

he would have created us that way."

~Koran

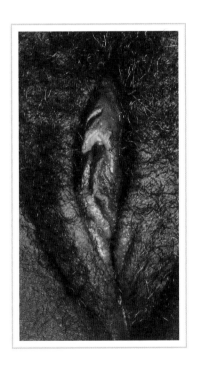
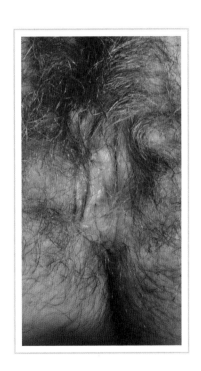
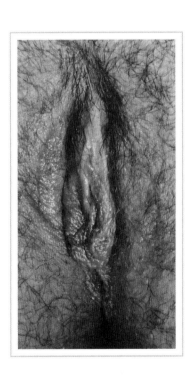

"It's all about falling in love with yourself and sharing that love with someone who appreciates you, rather than looking for love to compensate for a self love deficit."

~Eartha Kitt

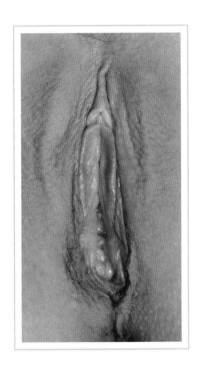 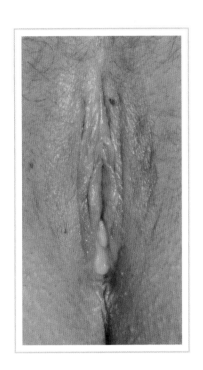 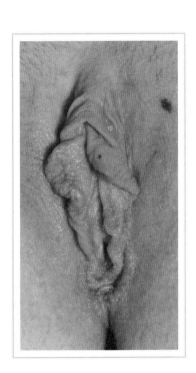

"When she stopped conforming to the conventional picture of femininity, she finally began to enjoy being a woman."

~Betty Friedan

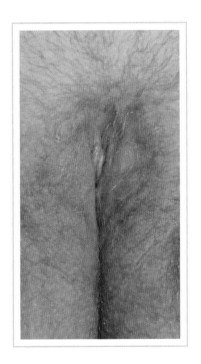 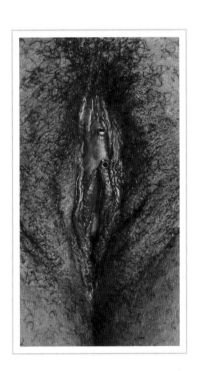 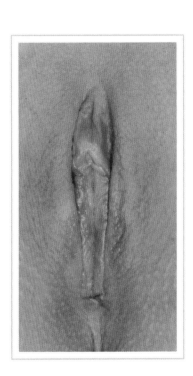

59

"Love is the great miracle cure.

Loving ourselves works miracles in our lives."

~Louise L. Hay

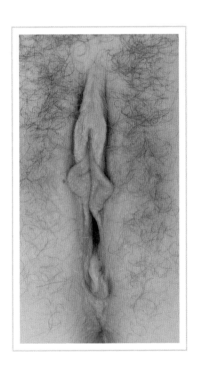 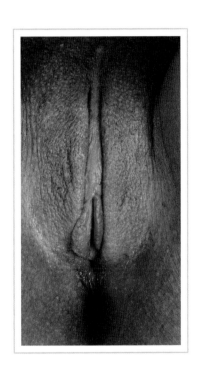 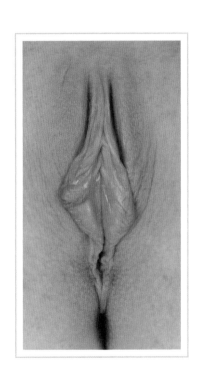

PETALS HISTORY

It all started with one woman complaining about how her vulva looked. She was Nick's lover at the time, and Nick simply wanted to show her how beautiful her vulva looked like to him. As a professional photographer and as a man who never doubted the powerful beauty of vulvas, Nick spent countless hours photographing her vulva and hand developing the film in his dark room. Many torn photographs later, she finally saw what Nick saw.

This woman then shared the photograph and her experience with a friend who also needed to see her own beauty. This friend was a member of an abused women's group, and many women from the group wanted to reclaim their genitals. Their vulvas and vaginas had become associated with pain and abuse, and many of these women wished their vulvas didn't exist at all. But they came to realize that denying their existence and beauty gave power to someone else, and they decided to be courageous and reclaim their vulvas! From that point on, the project took off via word of mouth. Before he knew what to do with them, Nick had photographed more than 100 women's vulvas.

With the strong encouragement of Nick's son Jesse, Nick's best friend and mentor Beck Peacock, and many of the women who posed for the photos, Nick decided to publish the images. In the beginning, he experimented with color photography. However, he noticed that most women were uncomfortable looking at color images and spent more time with the black and white photos. As an artist, he enjoyed working with black and white photographs. It was also very difficult for Nick to avoid making the color photos look like pornography. What he wanted to create was art, something people could take time with and meditate on. By changing all the photographs to sepia tone, the images were softened, and the result allowed more women to look at the images without feeling too vulnerable or objectified.

When none of the publishers Nick approached wanted to publish the book, Beck—at the time a film professor in San Diego—convinced Nick that the subject of Petals should be dug deeper and captured as a documentary film. "What is this discomfort around vulvas?" the two naïve men thought. "Vulvas are a natural part of women's bodies, they are gorgeous, they are powerful, they are the gateway of life. What are people's thoughts about vulvas and their beauty?" they wondered.

They travelled all over the United States and some parts of Canada interviewing and filming sex educators, sex therapists, cosmetic surgeons, art critics, and lay people to get a broad perspective. The journey captured Nick's struggle with the Petals project, the openness and transformation of women who participated in the project, as well as an actual Petals photo shoot. The end result is a moving, award-winning documentary that has been shown in more than 18 countries and become an official selection in more than 10 international film festivals.

Although the book was published in 2003, the documentary film Petals: The Journey into Self Discovery was not completed until 2008. Since the book's publication, Petals has been slowly gaining attention not only from individual women, but also by clinicians, sex therapists, healers, sex educators, and medical doctors.

As the audience for the film and the documentary grew, Nick started getting more and more requests for color images. Sexuality educators on the front lines told Nick and Sayaka that many women are not only concerned about the shapes of their vulva, but also the color. Most women's labia majora and labia minora are darker than the rest of their bodies, and some women worry they are not normal. We started asking around, and it was confirmed; many women think their vulva should have the same color as their skin, or should be soft pink. Our work was not complete, and it probably never will be, so it continues, with the Petals 2 in color! Viva la vulva!

WHY WE PUBLISHED THIS BOOK

We believe that nature created us all to be unique and beautiful. Yet many of us get stuck trying to achieve a standard of beauty that is unrealistic. In a world filled with new and improved beauty and cosmetic surgery techniques, the vulva might have been the last place you thought about in terms of beauty. Heck, we women have enough to worry about from head to toe, right? Yet, labiaplasty (cutting off the labia minora) and designer vaginas (including, but not limited to, vaginal tightening and G-spot enhancements) are fast becoming one of the most popular plastic surgeries in Australia, the UK, the United States, and possibly beyond.

Another concern is that many women have experienced some kind of sexual trauma. Our sacred part was (and maybe still is) the ground zero of our shame, pain, and anger. For this reason, many women feel disconnected from their genitals or carry emotional pain in and around the vulva and vagina.

Even if you have never experienced sexual trauma, most of us think of the vulva and vagina as an icky part of our body. Many women think it is dirty, yucky, and vulgar, something that needs to be cleaned often, not really looked at, touched, or appreciated, and somehow needs to look tidy and neat, and always smelling sweet.

Do you see something wrong with this picture? We do!

Our hope is that this book will help you have a better relationship with the sacred part of your body. We want you to admire the beauty, appreciate the scent and taste, marvel at the function, forgive it when it doesn't work as it "should," delight in the pleasure, give the respect it so deserves, and really, really love it! Our genitals are an honorable part of our body, not something dirty, disgusting, or humiliating, let alone something that needs to be cosmetically altered! Be proud, be unique, love yourself. We hope this book will help you get there, if not alone, then in conjunction with therapy, loving relationships, healing, and/or with other amazing books out there!

WHO MODELED FOR THE PHOTOS?

Everyone! They are professors, doctors, educators, students, activists, athletes, housewives, office workers, politicians, researchers, therapists, authors, actresses, healers, shamans, mothers, daughters, grandmothers, and goddesses. Their ages range from 19 to 73. They are mostly Americans from a variety of origins (Africa, Asia, Central America, South America, Europe, and the Middle East), but some are Canadian, Asian, European and Central American. Some of them identify themselves as queer, others as lesbian, bi-sexual, heterosexual, bi-curious, pan-sexual, goddess lover, and universal lover. Their sexual experiences range from only with themselves (self-identified virgin) to hundreds of partners. Many had some kind of sexual trauma; one woman experienced spousal rape and, as a result, had to undergo several vaginal reconstructive surgeries, while others had only consensual touch in and around their genitals. Most of them volunteered because they were moved by the original Petals book and the accompanying documentary. Others wanted to take back their genitals and reconnect and reintegrate this beautiful and amazing part of their body to their overall sense of self and well-being. Some were just curious, and others thought of this as "fun."

What they all had in common was the sense of empowerment and passion to help other women love themselves. We thank these amazingly brave women, who let us come so up close and personal, and trusted us to honor their images and use these images to heal and help women around the world.

ANATOMY AND PHYSIOLOGY

What most people define as a "vagina" actually consists of three major "Vs": vulva (the part you can see from the outside), vestibule (from the inner end of the labia minora to the entrance of vagina), and vagina (the inner canal to the cervix). A full diagram can be found below.

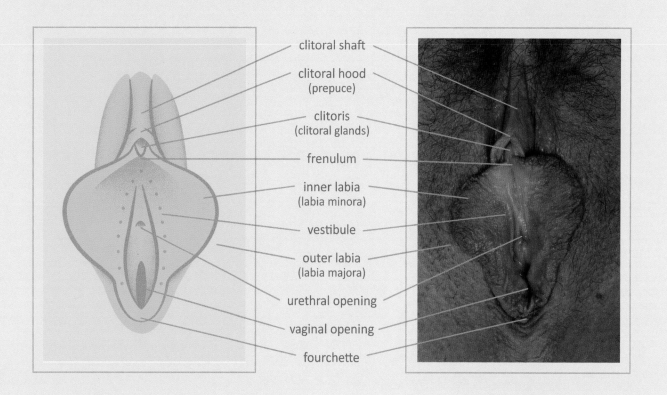

clitoral shaft

clitoral hood
(prepuce)

clitoris
(clitoral glands)

frenulum

inner labia
(labia minora)

vestibule

outer labia
(labia majora)

urethral opening

vaginal opening

fourchette

As you can see in the photographs, although we all have the same parts, our looks vary from woman to woman. Also, the same woman's "Vs" will look different from day to day, as well as at different states of arousal. So, check often and see how many faces and expressions your petals have!

One often overlooked vulva area is the vestibule. Most human sexuality and medical textbooks barely give mention to it, let alone discuss the differences among women. Some women have a smooth surface around the urethra and vaginal openings. Others, like the vulva pictured, have more intricate designs. While most women have their G-spot deep inside their vaginas, some women's G-spots are very close to the opening, sometimes protruding out to the vestibule. There is nothing wrong with that! In our experience, these women tend to ejaculate more easily than women whose G-spots are located deeper in their vagina.

Now, let's talk about the major players.

THE LABIA MAJORA, or outer labia, is the cushy part of our vulva that makes activities like sitting on a bike seat and intercourse more comfortable for us. It has hair follicles and sweat glans, so it's perfectly healthy that your yoga pants get wet during exercise. Don't worry, it does not cause "BO" like underarms. No deodorants needed.

The color and cushiness of the labia majora varies from woman to woman. Most of us have darker skin there, and when aroused, we get even darker, revealing the increased blood flow to the area.

THE LABIA MINORA, inner labia, or inner lips are rich in nerve endings and protect us from bacteria and viral invasions. During puberty, they grow larger and darker, just as boys' scrotums get darker and descend. Many girls are understandably freaked out by their labia minora's changes. They remember looking at themselves as little girls, maybe even playing doctor with other girls, and that's the image they have in their mind. Then, puberty hits, breasts start budding, hair starts growing, the menstrual cycle starts, all of which girls tend to be prepared for. But the inner labia also starts blossoming! Now, that's an unexpected event most girls are never prepared for. Many carry the shock with them for a long time, and if a sexual partner ever makes an unflattering comment, these girls often feel that there is something terribly wrong with their labia minora. They may look around to see if they are normal, but vulva images that are normally available are not good representations of normal, healthy vulvas. Just as smaller breasts are rarely seen on TV and in magazines, larger labia are rarely shown. As our vulva models reveal, labia minora that protrude to the outer labia are very common and perfectly normal. The next time you discuss the "birds and bees" with your daughters, please include this information to spare them from panic (and future labiaplasty)!

THE CLITORIS, often thought of as a small nub, is actually a pretty large structure. This is the only organ in our body whose sole purpose is creating pleasure. What is usually called the clitoris are actually the clitoral glans, the most nerve-packed, sensitive area of the clitoral structure. The clitoral shaft extends up toward the navel, from ¼ to more than one inch long, and under the clitoral hood (prepuce) it feels like a cord. Behind the clitoral hood, the clitoris splits into two, making a wishbone-shaped structure (crura) that extends down toward the vagina for about two inches.

The clitoral glans have thousands of nerve endings, making the area super sensitive. In fact, many women find it painful to touch the clitoral glans directly. If that's you, you can stimulate the glans over the prepuce or stimulate the shaft. Remember, the clitoris is a much bigger organ than just the glans! The whole clitoris engorges when aroused, and right before orgasm, it expands a bit more internally, making the clitoral glans disappear under the prepuce. Lots of people feel like they "lose" the clitoris at this time. Not to worry, just follow it upward and deeper, you will find it again!

THE G-SPOT, mostly unseen from the outside, became popular thanks to Beverly Whipple, John Perry, and Alice Ladas when they published the famous book The G-Spot and Other Recent Discoveries about Human Sexuality in 1982. After considering fun names like "Whipple Tickle," they decided to honor the German gynecologist and sex researcher Ernst Gräfenberg who first published about this area in the 1940s, thus naming it the Gräfenberg spot, in short, the G-Spot.

So what is it, anyway? The G-spot is a type of tissue surrounding the urethra (para urethra tissue or para urethra sponge) in the anterior wall of the vagina. Because it surrounds the urethra, when pressed, you feel like urinating. It is considered the female prostate, and it fills with prostatic fluid when aroused. This is how the G-spot can be easiest found; as it becomes aroused, it fills with fluid and becomes more rigid. The G-spot likes firm pressure, like a penis, also easily provided with fingers or toys. Have you heard that the "come hither" motion works well for the G-spot? It does, but most people don't go deep enough. Instead of doing the "come hither" motion on top of the G-spot, go deeper and press firmly, doing the motion at the back of the G-spot, kind of like trying to pull the whole thing toward the opening.

But, where does the G-spot fluid go? Most of the time, it gets sucked into and up the urethra and goes into the bladder. This is why most women have to use the bathroom right after sex. Other times, it travels to the urethra and comes out through the urethra opening. This fluid can be clear to very lightly milky white. The taste can be sweet to neutral, unlike the ammonia in urine. Most sexologists and researchers agree that when a woman is sufficiently aroused, she cannot urinate, just as a man usually cannot when he is aroused. G-spot fluid contains prostate specific androgen, showing that the fluid was made in a prostate gland. So, the next time you feel like urinating while rolling in the hay, put some extra towels down and let it go! You will most likely have a pretty good orgasm with the ejaculation, but some report that the orgasm and ejaculation are two separate events. If you don't ejaculate or find G-spot stimulation exciting, please don't worry. Actually, you are the majority. Only 30% of women have orgasms through penetration alone, while most others also require clitoral stimulation. So, whatever your pleasure, enjoy and don't make sex a competitive sport or another reason to feel insecure.

THE VAGINA is pretty amazing in its functions. It is a self-cleaning organ, so it does not need to be douched. The environment is acid, usually at a pH of 3.5 to 4.5, which helps kill any unwanted bacteria. The vagina also has its own culture of good bacteria, such as lactobacillus (yep, that yogurt thing), which keeps the vaginal flora happy. When you douche or take antibiotics, the good bacteria gets killed or disturbed, thus making you more susceptible to vaginal infections. Nature is pretty amazing, so let it do its job.

When you stand up, your vagina is not vertical, but rather tilts about 30 degrees toward your back. That's why it's helpful to push tampons in toward your back, instead of straight up. Normally, the vagina is like a collapsed balloon, unless it becomes aroused or something penetrates it. Its walls are made of soft tissue—rugae—like a pleated skirt, which stretches amazingly to accommodate a variety of sizes, including a baby!

When aroused, the rugae also expand, making the vaginal canal longer. As blood fills the vaginal walls, plasma from the blood seeps through the vaginal wall, making the vagina lubricate with clear, slippery beads. The amount of lubrication varies from woman to woman and from time to time. Take your time getting aroused, but don't worry if you are not as wet as you are "supposed to be." There is no such standard, and good water- or silicone-based lubricants are here to help you.

Now that you know about all the major parts of your genitals, get a mirror and identify all the parts. Get to know them, they are powerful and intoxicating part of you!

SCENT AND TASTE

Do you know what you smell like? Have you ever tasted yourself? You may be thinking, "Yack!" "Disgusting!" or "Are you kidding?" but there is nothing disgusting about it and we are not kidding. It is wonderful to get intimate with yourself, so you will know when your vulva is not happy and needs a doctor's attention.

What is a normal smell? You guessed it; it varies from person to person, from one time to another. Because our culture is so cleanliness obsessed and most of us were told that genitals are dirty, it is no wonder that people tend to find the genital's scent, or even talk of it, offensive. The truth is, because it's a self-cleansing organ, there is nothing dirty about our petals. Unless there is an infection, the vagina is the happiest when left to nature.

Get to know your scent and taste. Love it. Own it. Share it with the chosen partner(s). So many women try to mask the scent or worry about the taste. Make a decision to love your unique deliciousness. Your own scent can calm you, turn you on, and make you feel powerful. When your lover(s) tell you that you taste or smell good, believe them. This process may take a while, but it's definitely a worthwhile journey!

HOW TO KEEP THE PETALS HAPPY

1. Here are some easy things you can do to keep your petals happy.

2. Use mild detergent for your underwear, and rinse twice.

3. Whenever possible, go commando. Yep, petals love air.

4. When wearing underwear, go for the 100% cotton ones.

5. Avoid super tight jeans or anything that constricts the air and blood flow to your genitals. If you must wear them, wear for short periods and only occasionally.

6. Avoid fragrance down there. It is a source of irritation.

7. Avoid "deodorant" feminine products. If you are concerned about the smell, change your tampon or pad more often.

8. Only use panty liners when absolutely needed. Some discharge day-to-day is normal. Daily panty liner use will irritate your petals.

9. The glue in panty liners or sanitary napkins may irritate you. When you change them, also change your underwear so you don't come in contact with the glue.

10. Use the appropriate absorbency tampons, and only use super absorbency on your heaviest days. You want to keep the good moisture in your vagina.

11. Do not douche. Healthy bacteria need to stay in your vagina.

12. Wipe front to back, always.

13. When washing, use super mild soap (or just water) and run your finger between the labia majora and labia minora, all the way to the top of the clitoral hood and back. This area, called the interlabial sulcus, is hidden but still outside of the body and needs gentle washing. The labia minora, vestibule, and vagina don't need any special cleaning.

14. Only let clean hands and objects touch your vulva and vagina.

15. For sexual intercourse, wash before and after, use a male or female condom, and urinate immediately after.

And of course, please remember that your petals are a part of you. You always want to take care of yourself by eating well, exercising, being kind to yourself, managing stress, and accepting yourself fully.

PETALS PROBLEMS

Itchy? Red? Irritated? Painful? Bumps? Sores? Unusual smell or discharge? Although the vagina is self-cleaning and usually healthy, petals problems are not uncommon. What do you do when your petals are not happy?

First, look at yourself. Now that you know the proper anatomy, look through your petals and see which part is giving you concern. This will help your doctor help you when you see him or her.

Next, go to a doctor. You might be afraid of being judged, embarrassed for your condition, or just plain hate doctor's visits. You may want to self-diagnose and treat your symptoms with over-the-counter remedies, but unless you've had the same condition before and are absolutely sure it's the same thing, you need to see a doctor.

Good doctors will not judge you; they have seen and heard it all, and they are compassionate. Of course, like anyone, doctors are humans and sometimes, you may not jive with one of them. If so, check with another doctor. It's very important that you feel comfortable with your doctor; they are one of our most important petals confidants! A good doctor will help you understand your petals deeper instead of making you feel shame or guilt. If you haven't found the right doctor yet, don't give up! Ask your friends, check out online reviews, and keep trying. When you find that fantastic, compassionate doctor, you will be so glad you didn't give up searching.

WANT MORE?

To join the I Love My Petals community, please join us on Facebook:
www.facebook.com/ilovemypetals

For more information on female empowerment, vulva and vagina resources,
and great book recommendations, please visit us at:
www.ilovemypetals.com